Along the Fifty Fathom Line

Deep Sea Poems

BY

R A Bard

Expanded Edition

January 2019

Copyright Smooth Passage Books

Table of Contents

THE KESTREL

Eighty-five miles off the beach
With a waypoint entered for home
Cruising through heavy grey mist
Grey the seas, grey the sky, grey the foam

The cabin is warm, and the engine's hum
Drones on, leads us into a kind
Of torpor, an easy continuum
The season's travails left behind

When suddenly there's a flurry,
A panic of wings off the bow
It's a sparrow hawk, lost in the fog
And trying to figure out how

To perch on this alien platform
That rolls back and forth in the swell
From the mast, to the pole, to the gunwale
It flits, then flies off for a spell

Till at last the exhausted bird lights
On the foredeck, just in from the rail
And ruffs up its feathers, and hunches
As on through the grayness we sail

Now a headwind is throwing up spray
That's soaking the hawk where it stands
And as time passes by it's collapsing
Its fate, I see, rests in my hands

I creep forward, holding a towel
Optimistically thinking I could
Wrap it up and convey it inside
Where the warmth might do it some good

But just as I'm ready to move
It senses me, springs up in fright
And, frantic, collides with a backstay
And plummets astern, out of sight

I run aft, but nothing is there
Just the wake fading into the fog
So I toss the towel into the cabin
And gaze around, sick as a dog

At this tragedy. But now a ruckus
Erupts from just inside the door
Where the hawk, who'd flown in for safety
Was knocked by my towel to the floor

It's not hurt, and after a struggle
I get it set up on a pile
Of rope I've arranged as a perch
Where it's dry. At last I can smile

And go back to the drone of the engine
And my dreams of the summer that's flown
As the lids of the hawk, too, grow heavy
And it nods off to dreams of its own

Hours go by in this reverie
As we gradually bear in toward shore
Then, at forty miles off, the hawk wakes
And hops down to stand by the door

And fixes my gaze for a moment
Then purposefully leaps into flight
By the time I get back to look out
It's gone in the fog, out of sight.

Hawk, it's forty miles over the waves
Before you can cross to the coast
If your strength doesn't flag it should take you
Two hours or three at the most---

May your sixth sense plot a true course;
May you daydream of shore as you fly
Of a perch in the sun, by a field full of mice,
And of updrafts in clear warm blue sky.

RITE OF WAY

The skipper called the new hand up to the wheel.
Said, "how ya doin', kid, think you can drive a boat like this?"
"Not sure," says Rolf. "I'm not sure if I feel---"
"Nothin' to it, really, stay alert and you can't miss.

Here's the plotter here's the compass
Here's the pilot here's the throttle
Keep the cursor on the A-B
Line right here, there's not a lot'll

Trip you up. I gotta rest I'm on my thirteenth cup of coffee
Though it's barely been three hours since I let the mate go off, he'd
Been standin' at the helm straight through from four to midnight
And I knew he'd be a wreck so even though I'm still wound uptight

From not sleepin', from the stress of tryin' to get these fish to town
Before this storm hits and the fleet runs in and knocks the dock price
down
With 20 tons of black cod here we've got a lot to lose
Instead of smilin' at the bank we'd just be blubberin' the blues

So I gotta get some sleep---just an hour or two
Till I get caught up, then I'll come and take her back
Remember, move to starboard is what you wanna do
If a boat is comin' at you and you're on the same track

Port to port, that's red to red
Is how you want to pass her
Here's the radar, here's the jogstick,
turns us port or starboard. Yassir

Then, sport, I don't see too much congestion
But I'm right there in my stateroom if you got the slightest question."
The captain hit the rack, leaving Rolf a deer in a spotlight
Peering into the pre-storm black of the Southeast Alaska night

With a total previous history of about two hours steering
And that in broad daylight---now, with confidence disappearing
With minimal expertise, and with zero frame of reference
He hurtles into the vast and dark expanse of Dixon Entrance

There isn't the smallest comforting glimmer of light out there anywhere
And Rolf gets an unwanted flashback of his mom, and a teddy bear
But there's no bear here, just a roaring Cat in this 60-foot longliner
And 20 tons of black cod. Well, our man Rolf's no whiner

And after a bit he starts to check out the radar, the plotter, the charts---
Well, here's Cape Chacon, there's Rose Spit, and down there Chatham
Sound starts...
Here's the course line the skipper set---It's starting to make some sense
And sitting there in the pilot's chair, he gathers confidence

And before long he's become Rolf the Mighty Helmsman
The course is set, the coast is clear---hey, this is kinda fat!
Rolf pulls out his iPod and cues up a selection
A bit of fishy smelling rap by Snoop Channel Cat---

Toes two timin in my Xtra tuffs
Feel the heat on the street while I'm chasin down muff
I'm the squeakin wheel that's gettin the grease
Come up short, go report it to the pelt police
A tight piece of candy on the arm is no harm
Dealing highs, well don't send me to no prison farm

Take that Manafort con, made the cash disappear
To the fat cat's pocket in the election year
He'll do time, yeah right when the sun turns green
Special prosecutor part of the same machine
Blood on those suits that won't never come clean
But the faces are grey, ain't no high in that scene
Off that CNN, better turn up the sounds
Wipe the frown, kick it down to the ground, hit the town
Don't let the creeps drive you round that bend
Cause livin large---that's the best revenge

The beat's got to Rolf, he's in a near hypnotic state
His face ginned up with an oblivious smirk
When intruding on his reverie, a sense of impending fate
Punches out the hiphop muse, and he comes to with a jerk

What's this now we're looking at, a whole city up ahead
But what's that on the edges, a green light and a red
That can't be Prince Rupert, we're still forty miles away
Could that be another boat, all lit up as bright as day?

Let's see---and Rolf peers into the radar screen
Counts four rings up to a big green splotch
That's closing so fast Rolf too turns kinda green
Shit! How come I'm the one that's gotta be on watch?

Calm down now, keep it cool
Think what the skipper said
How'd it go now, come on, fool---
Damn---oh yeah, red to red!

Pass his port light on our port, that's how I want to take it
I'll just come to starboard, let's see, twelve degrees should make it
That looks good, the radar course line's well off to his right
Whew, that was close, I don't want to get in a fight

With a boat that size, look at all those lights, it's a cruise ship I'll just bet
A geezer liner full of folks from Ohio, playing roulette,
Eating king crab and drinking margaritas---hey, that'd be pretty slick---
On the other hand, maybe they're all just miserably seasick...

This line of thought which could have led to existential dread
Gets cut short as Rolf, with a sinking in his gut
Sees the ship is once again directly dead ahead---
Oh my god---didn't turn far enough, now I'd better cut

The crap and get us turning
To starboard in a hurry
Cause this guy is really burning
And so Rolf in a flurry

Of action cuts the pilot, puts his back into the wheel
Gives it thirty degrees this time, which for a moment lets him feel
Some relief, until he finds that the red light is gone, oh how
Am I gonna get past to his port---he's right in front of me now---

Rolf cranks hard right but the horrible circus of light refuses to pass
On the radar a large and a much smaller blip merge and form one sickly
green mass
Rolf tries to yell for the skipper---the cry gets stuck in his throat
One last yank on the wheel is all he can do in his final few seconds
afloat

The green light goes out... a white light appears...
And Rolf's eyes see, through fought-back tears
The stern light of the cruise ship receding to the west
And he stands transfixed---by God, I must be blessed.

The boat, its wheel still over, makes a full revolution
And yet one more before Rolf finally shakes off his confusion
And straightens out her heading on the former compass course
And, trying to dig himself out of a quagmire of remorse

Steers by hand for two straight hours, till he hears the skipper's voice
Say "How'd it go, kid?" leaving him to make a choice
As to how much of the truth his answer should allow
In the end decides truth is kinda relative, anyhow...

"Not bad---saw one other vessel
Passed us going the other way.
That was it. Well, now I guess I'll
Go below if that's okay."

"You bet, and thanks for taking the watch, it helped a lot."
As Rolf turns in, the skipper checks out the plotter. Well, what've we got---
He did fine, track line's straight but for this little nick
Still on the fifty mile range, though, I'll just zero in real quick

Hits the button and zooms to the ten mile range, five, two and a half
Eyes the two donuts they'd turned twelve miles back, gives out a small puzzled laugh
The hell's up with this, tryin' to make art on the plotter, thinks he's Toulouse Lautrec?
I should blister his ass!---but I'll just let it pass. He's way too good out on deck.

COMMUNION

This really happened
I swear, this really happened
If you need corroboration
You can ask a former deckhand
Although his testimony
Mighty be viewed as unreliable
Since almost his last words to me
Were that commonly offered advice
That starts out with "fuck"
And finishes with "you"
Delivered at great volume
When he'd itemized a list
Of real and made-up grievances
He'd suffered at my hands
Through the prior month of fishing
And followed by demands
That he be taken back to port
Because he wasn't going to put up
With this bullshit any longer
Which was how, crewless in Sitka
I came to rescue Vern
From a pair of Shee Atika sirens
Who, in two feverish nights
Had relieved him of the burden
Of three months of fishing pay
Leaving him with nothing
But a half a pint of Irish
And a bag of sour sweatshirts---

But that's another story.
Skipping back a month in time

To when Jim and I were cordial
There were coho in abundance
In the mouth of Sitka Sound
At the finish of a dreamy day
On a gently rolling ocean
With the sun descending slowly
Through some rose colored clouds
We pulled the gear aboard
To drift for the night
Curiously, in the middle
Of a great school of porpoise
Maybe several hundred strong
Doing that slow, humping roll
They'll sometimes exhibit
When feeling contemplative
Or possibly just lazy

As Jim was fixing dinner
I took out my recorder
A soprano that I'd given
To my kids and stolen back
Because my alto wasn't near as good
For playing with a diesel
You just can't get the volume
And the registers conflict
So I took this little Yamaha
Out into the sunset
And sat down on the hatch cover
And tried to reproduce a sound
I thought dolphins might credit:
A squeaky, skwirling, high pitched riff
Like a desperate sax might blow
Trying to rise above the murk
Of a smoky club, on an offbeat night---

It wasn't what they wanted.
Before the last note faded
The entire audience dove as one
Retreated several boat lengths north.
Disdain hung heavy in the air
As if, portraying Hamlet
Some misdirected actor
Had delivered the soliloquy
Entirely in pig latin.

I sucked some spit out of the mouthpiece
Tried again with Bach's
Jesu, Joy of Man's Desiring:

Measured and patient progressions that if you allow it
can carry you
through all the static that builds up
from life's disillusionments finding and
laying bare still vital caches of calm understanding
And hope for the
future that gladdens and lifts up your soul.

At least that's what it does for me sometimes
As it must have done for the porpoise
Cause I swear they all came back
Within yards of the boat,
Once more rolling slowly
And after I finished
It was exceptionally quiet
Until a single whiteside porpoise
Stood on its head
And beat the water's surface
For a full ten seconds
With its tail.

I've often wondered, since that night
What really happened there
What's the sound of one tail clapping?
Was it as it seemed, applause?
I'm certain they were listening
And although I want to think
They were tuned in to the harmony
I can't really say---
It's too great a leap of faith
In the same way that religion
Always has eluded.

Does a dolphin dream of heaven?
Pray to a flippered god?
Or is living immersed in nature
Paradise enough?

REPRISE   (for the foundered fisherman)

You can make a kind of living
As a gleaner even yet
You can take a roadside harvest
Of aluminum cans
You can hedge around the edges
Of futures trading floors
And profit off the residue
Of each miscalculation
You can still catch remnant salmon
Progress hasn't yet extinguished...

I do my gleaning now
In the spiritual field,
Finding glory in the leavings
Of those with faith so strong
It lives on, clear and vibrant
In the music they created
As in Handel's Messiah
As in the Bach Cantatas
Vivaldi's flute concertos;
Their overpowering rapture
Can fill the deepest hunger
When their passions roll across me
Past the intervening years
I am reverently thankful
That I was born with ears.

FARMED FISH

I may have been chasing salmon around
For more than twenty years
But that doesn't mean I've got no more
Than wax between my ears.
If it's tougher to make a living,
I can find experts to tell me why
And the expert advice is, to stay afloat
I've got to diversify.

You drive a deckload up to the dock
For what used to be major pay
The buyer looks down, and snickers, and snorts,
And tells you to go away
No matter how low your price, the farmers
In Norway are asking far less
And Chile will sell for half of that,
And they ship by Federal Express.

As the price goes down, the volume must rise
So you're working double time
You're in the pit from dark till dark
And up to your beard in slime
And though you know hard work's no crime,
And never has brought you harm
For this much dough, you might as well go
Get a job on a chicken farm.

We've got to join the marketplace! We've got to value-add!
We had our good days in the past, but now we're just being had.
It's time to value-add, my friends! It's time to learn to sell!
We'll stand up tall to the middleman and sternly bow: Farewell!

We've got to vertically integrate,
And horizontal too.
Instead of sticking just to fishing,
We'll process like others do---
We'll head and gut and skin and fletch
And steak and debone and fillet
And bread and batter and pickle and salt
And blacken the Cajun way
We'll shred and compress! We'll mince and bind!
Dehydrate and liquefy

We'll freeze and refresh and boil and bake
And steam and saute (or fry)
We'll bag, and seal, and box, and can,
And wrap and vacuum pack
And then we'll dig out our contacts list
And get on the marketing track

We'll haggle and wheedle, flatter and needle;
Consult and cajole and conspire
Call in some favors and give out some freebies,
Whatever the deal might require
We'll put on an ad blitz in Paris and Biarritz
And Rome and Vienna and Moscow
Then, just to ensure that we cover all bases
We'll penetrate Walmart and Costco

We'll network with chefs from white tablecloth rooms
And befriend institutional buyers
We'll take to the air and we'll jet everywhere,
And beyond, and become frequent fliers
We'll get to know Avis and Budget and Hertz
And Ramada and Holiday Inn
And learn to like airline food, peanuts and pretzels
And Maalox and Ibuphrophen

And sooner or later we'll come out on top,
If only we persevere
And then we can boast to all the world,
In a way that's perfectly clear
How it feels to finally gain the success
For which we've so long been wishing
By a sticker, proudly affixed to our car,
With the legend:

I'D RATHER BE FISHING

Big Business

I had a dream the other night
Or, rather, it had me
In what was sure a glimpse of hell
I dreamt a violent fate befell
Those who in small boats brave the swell
To fish the northern sea.

A giant fleet of factory boats
Had spread out off the coast
Down from marine ways far and wide
From Mobile to Taipei they'd slide
And, once afloat, with others vied
For which would catch the most.

They floated on shoals of bankers' notes
And the toil of women and men
Six on, six off, around the clock
For months, till when they hit the dock
They'd swiftly spend their pay, then flock
To sign up once again.

The deadly strength of the factory fleet
Began to turn the screw
The pollock schools, at first immense
Became, with time, not near as dense
Until, with fearful imminence
Their end came into view.

The growing glut of hungry ships
To other groundfish veered
And one by one these other stocks---
Pacific cod, and perch, then rocks---
Like mice in jaws of hungry fox
Each gasped and disappeared.

The time had long since come and gone
To slow from run to crawl
But caution is of small avail
When investment's on so huge a scale
Investment pressure would prevail;
Nothing could stop the trawl.

Executives skyped through day and night
Their cell phones buzzed away
The Fisheries Management Council met;
The factories' spokesmen labored to get
Their point across, and the Council let
The giant fleet have its way:

No longer would salmon and halibut
And black cod be reserved
For smaller craft. The monstrous raft
Of factories loosed the nets abaft
And gleefully the skippers laughed
As through those schools they swerved.

In Bering Sea and Alaskan Gulf
More stocks began to fall.
First halibut, then sables waned;
The salmon, swifter, still retained
Some hope, but the mighty engines strained
And the nets enclosed them all.

Strangely, smaller boats still thrived
On what few fish remained
Around the rockpiles near the beach
In where the factories couldn't reach
Where snags their nets would surely breach
Some balance was maintained.

Offshore, the nets sieved emptiness
The cod ends came up bare
And soon the banks and businessmen
Convened the Council yet again
But reapportionment's no use when
There are no fish to share.

Now lawyers sharp in bankruptcy
Began to circle round.
Collapse seemed near for the factory fleet
But one brave manager stood from his seat
And spoke with such righteous, fervent heat
That the doomsayers' talk was drowned.

"There's plenty of resource yet, my friends
Our future still is bright
Demand for wood in Korea is real
And Chinese factories hunger for steel
If we drag for boats, we can cut quite a deal
Necessity makes it our right."

So the factories shot once more their nets
And aimed for the inshore fleet
And longliners, gillnetters, trollers, all
Saw hulls collapse and rigging fall
As each was caught in a crushing trawl
And processed like so much meat.

And then I awoke. In catharsis I smiled---
Just a nightmarish dream of a kind.
I thought the moon full, for the porthole was bright,
Lit from outside---but wait, it's an overcast night,
And what's that dark shape, with huge sodium light
Coming up on us fast from behind?

THE KING OF NO DEAD BIRDS

You're on the midnight wheel watch, you make this simple move
Reach up and turn two toggle switches off
Suddenly the world ahead is plunged into darkness.

You glance around behind you, you give a nervous cough,
You wonder if the hammer's coming down
Cause those sodiums are always on when under way at night.

Though the genset doesn't need the load, and no one's gonna drown
It's the plotter and the radar that keep you off the rocks.
The lights are there for finding gear, to light the working deck.

But that's not happening now; you're just heading for the docks
In Akutan---a fifty-hour run down the chain
You know the route; the skipper laid it out on the plotter;

And you know what'd likely happen in three miles as you maintain
This course that takes you past an offshore reef
Where seabird flocks in countless numbers raft through the night.

You're all too well acquainted with the sense of needless grief
When they all rise up, freaked out by the lights
And circle frantically around: the fulmars fluttering wildly

Murres and auklets arcing past in crazy erratic flights
Puffins streaking by, like misdirected rockets
And, throughout, the thumps as blinded birds hit the rigging.

In the morning they're all over the deck, with wings jammed out of sockets
Broken necks, and worse, you find the wounded and the dead
Scattered, in the dozens. And you and the rest of the crew

Would gather them up, and callously, it has to be said,
You throw them overboard like so much trash.
Now you're hardly a vegan, you understand life is rough,

That killing's part of the things you do, to earn your share of cash
But killing fish is one thing; and this is, simply, wrong
And so you've resolved, it won't happen while you're on watch

You may catch hell from the skipper, might be asked to move along
To another boat---but for now that's just speculation
For now, you're simply content to be: the king of no dead birds.

ANOTHER TRIP ON THE FACTORY SHIP

The night before Christmas, and all through the trawler
The crew's morale level had never been smaller.
Since June, when we'd left for a two-month-long trip
A jinx had been squatting on our hapless ship.

The pollock eluded; the gray cod weren't there;
There seemed to be no fish for us anywhere.
Oh, we picked up the odd haul, but mostly caught water.
Might as well have had Saskatoon plugged in the plotter.

Christmas Day in the Donut Hole---what could be sadder?
What could was when Charlie got sucked in the Baader
His boombox went, too, and CD of Metallica
And his "sea cucum" T-shirt (too blatantly phallic). Uh---

Maybe that's why we just stood there like stumps
As the razor-sharp blades carved him deftly to lumps
Filleted him and processed him, on down the line,
Through mincers and grinders that chopped him up fine.

Just when Chuck had been mixed with the other surimi,
The Captain's voice rattled us out of our dreamy
Trance, grumbling, "Damn! What an unlucky quirk!
Well, nothing to do 'bout it now. Back to work!"

So we finished the trip out and headed for port
Disheartened at how low our shares would be short
But when we'd unloaded, we sent up a holler---
The buyers went crazy. The load fetched top dollar!

The taste, they pronounced so good as to amaze
They'd not, since the good orange roughy days,
Had a product so marketable. We cheered our luck,
Retracted a bit of our snideness toward Chuck.

Now we're fishing again. We had two days ashore!
I partied till my party muscles were sore.
Then I went out and bought me a brand new Toyota.
Happy Groundhog to all! And to all a big quota!

THE KETA HAPPINESS

All winter long we dipped from the freezer
The catch that we'd saved from last season
And thankful we were, for to chew on a fish
And look back on the summer's right pleasin'

The kings of July were the first ones to go
Like that big white we caught off Cape Chacon
We broiled it one fine autumn night on the grate
And lay back in the grass, our lips smackin'

We baked up another on Thanksgiving Day
When the grandfolks from back East came wobblin'
It wasn't a turkey; Halloween was long gone,
But still there was plenty of gobblin'

The silvers we sauteed at Christmas
The humpies went stir-fry 'round New Year
With ling cod we chowdered and deep-fried our way
Through the next month---and, finally, spring's near

But, hell. It's still March, the unkindest of months
When the promise of warmth stays denied
And the winter winds, kicked up for one final blow
Do their best to fillet off your hide

And boat work's at hand, though the weather's still foul
And the money's near gone, and the creditors howl
And the garden patch, it's still too sodden to trowel
What we need is a fish to stay March's mad growl---

But we've eaten them all. Even the bomber
We fried it for tacos last weekend
Still, just out of hope I go back to the chest
And rummage 'round down in the deep end

And there you are, under the ice cubes and bread
The dog that all winter we'd spurned
But that's just how it seemed---it was you, all along!
It was you for whom, truly, we'd yearned.

We'd got you last fall from an old packer friend
He said you were bright (I knew better)
No sweat, though. I carry you out to the grate
Wearing three flannel shirts and a sweater

Lay you over the embers and grill you up right
With garlic and ginger and butter
Take you back to the family inside. We dig in.
Our contentment is too great to utter.

Now your skeleton lies in the weeds by the grill
And I'm picking my teeth, still struck dumb
Till the gratitude wells up, and I burp it out:
"You were wonderful. So long, old chum."

(*Onchorynchus Keta* = "dog" = "chum" salmon)

WHAT A DRAG

Beat up, and tired, and making scant headway
We shouldered our way through a steep brutal chop
After stacking the troll gear on deck for the day
When the oncoming night brought our work to a stop

Though I would have stopped sooner, if I'd any sense
If I'd hadn't been so distracted with greed
I'd have quit well before the seas grew so intense
As to make the boat jerk like a whippet on speed

First her bow scraped the sky, then her port rail rolled under
A stabie got flipped fifteen feet in the air
A wave top crashed over the transom like thunder
And filled up our boots---but we didn't much care

Cause throughout this chaos the silvers were biting,
Were schooled up and hungry---how couldn't I stay?
Though the rest of the fleet long ago gave up fighting
The weather and took off for Yakutat Bay

Six hours to Ocean Cape, one more beyond
And you're into the lee there, behind Point Carew
And anchored in water as still as a pond
You can sleep like a child the entire night through

Whereas along this coast, far as Cape Fairweather
There isn't so much as a bight to tuck in
Just a handful of rivers; no use wondering whether
To shelter there---shallow bars, rougher than sin

But what we could do is get close to the shore
And hope that the land knocked the wind down a notch
Cause a six-hour run to the Bay'd make it four
In the morning before we'd at last go off watch...

For an hour...till time to start fishing again...
Forget it, I said, we'll just give this a shot.
The forecast's for calming by morning, and when
We get up we'll be anchored just inside the spot

Where the fish are, instead of a long buck away.
So I motored on in to eight fathoms and stopped,
Made my way to the bow, where I clung to a stay
And undogged the anchor and watched as it dropped

Swiftly into the dark water under the bow,
Ran out with a scream fifteen fathoms of chain,
Twenty more of stout nylon, and more, cable now,
Then I dogged off the winch and stared into the rain.

The wind felt like thirty, the seas eight to ten
With no sign of light anywhere in the sky
Calm there might be in store, but I couldn't say when
The forecast was calm, but I couldn't see why.

The anchor caught hold, the bow swung with a jerk
The troller leaped up and faced into the breeze
Took hold of her bridle and got down to work
As if by bucking violently, she might appease

Some malevolent god that knew nothing but hell.
I groped to the wheelhouse, went inside to gaze
At the plotter, while from the galley a smell
Of hot stew set my appetite gladly ablaze

Then I saw, from our rapidly lengthening track
We had dragged, already a tenth of a mile
And were still falling off, and I'd have to go back
To the bow once again; dinner'd wait for a while.

Back on with the rain gear, back into the blow
I reeled in the whole line, in case it was foul,
Let it back out, and more, twenty fathoms or so,
Got it set and dogged off with a curse and a growl.

Back inside, I'd nearly finished my meal
When a look at the screen caused my stomach to sink
We were dragging again. This was getting unreal
I pulled on my raincoat, tried hard not to think

About all the places I'd rather have been,
Forced myself out into the wind and the spray
And in one final effort to dig the flukes in
Unbraked and paid cable out, all the way

Leaving only one wrap on the end of the spool.
Eighty fathoms of line in eight fathoms of water:
If this didn't work, maybe I was a fool
To be here. I ducked back inside to the plotter

And glared at the cursor. By God, there it stayed
In one spot. I slowly came out of my funk,
Ran a brush past my teeth, and then wearily made
My last safety checks, and crawled into my bunk

And I tried to drift off. And I utterly failed.
Cause the boat had turned into a carnival ride
Pitching wildly, and crashing, and sometimes she'd sail
Cross the wind far enough to get rolled on her side

Which, of course, meant I'd roll up onto the wall
And come flopping back down. Meanwhile, the noise factor,
The clatter of loose pans and spare parts and all
Was like being inside a garbage compactor.

But at last I dozed off. At least, so I assume
Because something awoke me at just before two.
It was eerie, the relative calm in the room
We were rolling much less, and it seemed we'd come through

To the end of the blow. Still, the wind was as strong,
Or yet stronger, to judge by the roar from outside.
I crept from the bunk, certain something was wrong
I looked at the plotter, and I almost cried.

Four miles of track line shone there on the screen.
I tried to remember how badly I'd sinned
To deserve this---just one thing that track line could mean:
The anchor was gone; we were sailing downwind.

I pulled on my oilskins, and then took a light
Out to spool in what anchor line might still remain
And found, to my wonder, the cable still tight:
We were dragging, not drifting, and that would explain

Why the boat's motion seemed so much easier now:
While we coasted along, with the wind and the tide,
The anchor still pulled hard enough on the bow
It rode into the seas, giving us a smooth ride.

I went back inside, and I checked the depth meter
Eight fathoms, exactly where we'd started out.
I looked at our plot line, it couldn't be neater
Parallel to the coast and a half a mile out.

The radar showed no other boats within range.
Six hours to run to the Bay? I'd be dead.
I set an alarm to sound any depth change,
And then, "Screw it," I said, and I went back to bed.

The rivers slipped by as we dragged past the Dangerous
Past the Italio, the Lost, and the Situk
Dragged toward whatever fate might hold in store for us
Riding the waves like a napping sea duck

Or an idiot, I'm still not sure which applies
All I know is the new day finally dawned
And I got up, rubbing the sleep from my eyes
And turned up the plotter, while widely I yawned

And then I stepped back, full amazed at the sight
Of the track line that shone there, as straight as an arrow
Eighteen miles we had dragged, through that short stormy night
I felt like a fool---and I felt like a pharaoh.

Eighteen miles dragging anchor: was this a bold stroke,
A feat to proclaim, like some great baseball stat?
Or a sign of a brain account fast going broke
A blunder I ought to keep under my hat...

We fished that day; I don't recall what we caught
My eyeballs felt like they were filled up with tar
But since then, there's many a time that I've thought
That I ought to get clear about dragging so far

So I'm claiming the record---and claiming it proud.
Don't care if some say I'm a knothead to brag
'Cause at bottom, the eighteen-mile furrow we plowed
Through that night, was surely one hell of a drag.

THE TOURIST

I was grumbling down the dock
With the early season blues
When---damn! Here comes a tourist
Wearing flashy running shoes

And some peg leg Levis
And a slick leather coat
And he'd got me in his sights
As I was heading for my boat

I was weathered in the harbor
Wishing I was home
In zero mood for trash talk
With some simple minded gnome

But his "Hey, how you doing?"
Rang unwelcome in my ear
"Boy, look at all these boats!"
"How come they're all in here?"

I knew, declining groundfish
Was a good part of the reason
And with crab becoming scarcer
At this stage of the season

Getting knocked around for nothing
Wasn't worth the struggle
Best to find some warm companion
And stay at home and snuggle

Wait for a calmer day.
But it wasn't worth my time
Explaining to this halfwit
So I shrugged and walked away

But he stayed right at my side
Nothing, if not persistent
And he launched some crazy story
In a voice loud and insistent

He was a white collar worker
A civil engineer no less
Married, with some kids,
Then he started to regress

One day, he just flipped out
Couldn't take it any more
Told his wife he'd had enough
And walked right out the door

Found himself a different job
Off in another state
Made some friends, sent money home
Seemed things were going great

But then it fell apart again
He got a DUI...
Told his boss to shove the job
---he couldn't stand the guy---

Had to move out of his house
Had no other place to live
Wore his welcome out with friends
Then, with no rent money to give

Joined the other down and outs
With a bunk at the Gospel Mission.
Sunk that low, he got the thought
If he could just go fishin'

Everything would straighten up
"So!" he says to me. "How 'bout it?
Know somebody needing crew?
I'd be good, and don't you doubt it."

But he kinda had the shakes
And doubt was all I had
I was looking for a deckhand
But he was looking bad

He was (1) living like a bum
(2) had a giant monkey drinking---
This is one to stay away from
Is what my mind was thinking

But my mouth said, well, let's see
I'll give it a little thought
Check back in a couple days
Could be I'll have a spot

I thought I'd have no worries,
I was sure he'd never show
Two days later, though, he shambles
Down the dock and says "Let's go!"

Tried my best to steer him off
Told him every miserable thing
You run into when you fish
From lack of sleep to jelly stings

Carpal tunnel, long hard hours
Blood and scales and slime and guts
Days and days without a shower
Aching back and leader cuts

Scrubbing, cooking, cleaning, icing
Starting before break of day
Lumpy seas that make you barf
Grouchy skippers, lousy pay

I worked so hard to turn him off
I got *myself* into a funk
Man! I thought, this just sounds awful!
Maybe *I* should go get drunk...

He remained enthusiastic
Said he'd handle what came down
So I gave in, signed him on
Certain I'd just hired a clown

I dug out some ragged raingear
Figured he could use
He bought goofy yellow rubbers
That snapped outside his shoes

And so we set out, this weird pair
Grumpy veteran and Mr. Green
Across the bar and into the ocean
And---the strangest thing I've seen

He seemed born to be a sailor
Never close to getting sick
The raft of things he didn't know,
He had no trouble learning, quick

Got the basic duties easy
At handling fish he was first rate
Read the electronics manuals
Taught himself to navigate

Best of all, he wasn't one
To idly sit around and stew
Even when fishing was slow
He'd look around for something to do

So we put in a month of fishing
Out on the banks above Coos Bay
The salmon were few, the weather a bear
But we worked hard and made it pay

Then headed north up to Alaska
And the heart of the season for kings
The opening day I'll always remember
As one of my favorite things

Somehow I managed to put us
On a huge school of hungry chinook
Starting when we first dropped in
Big salmon on every hook

Through the day it went like that
A silver glittering flood
Soon our muscles were aching
Faces covered with blood

The tourist held up his end
Through a pace completely berserk
At one point he did hit the wall
But he bounced and got back to work

And that's how the whole season went
I couldn't escape from the fish
Every time I made a move
I was granted my fondest wish

And the tourist kept up with it all
Though I caught more than ever before
He got them all iced down in the hold
No matter how high the day's score

I won't say he was perfection
One flaw I'm compelled to report
His love of the juice meant he'd cut loose
Whenever we went into port

We'd tie up, he'd zoom up the dock
Toward Rosie's, the P-Bar, Glass Door
Pulling teeth, it was to get help
With groceries or some other chore

Sometimes I had to wait hours
Till he showed up, to head back to sea
But I never complained too hard
He was too much an asset to me

And in one way, I could understand
At least one reason he drank
Though not quite God's gift to women
When he'd put in two thirds of a tank

The fairer sex couldn't resist him
He found girlfriends wherever we went
(Except Yakutat---but scoring there
Only happens by accident).

By the time we got to September
And the season ran out of gas
I'd landed my highest catch ever.
Heading home through Cameron Pass

For the first time in years I was flush.
And though he'd tried to drink it away
Even my deckhand had saved up
Enough bucks for some rainy day

We punched our way south toward home
I considered the moral I'd learned
You make snap judgments on people
Chances are, you'll get burned

You can't judge a book by its cover
A man's more than how he is dressed
You write off a guy by the look in his eye
You'll never see him at his best

I last saw my man in the Islands
Just north of Puget Sound
We were cruising past Galiano
When he says, hey, slow down

I'll catch a ferry in to Vancouver
And go see my family there
Give them a share of my earnings
Yeah, that's what would be fair.

He tried a few more resolutions
Said maybe he'd give up the booze
Quit smoking, get on the straight track
Abandon these wandering blues

He dropped to the float with his bags
Said, it's been a good one, hey skip?
That's no lie, I said, and cast off
As he walked back into his trip

Then I saw, at the head of the dock
A bar, looking friendly as hell
Which way he turned at its door...
I don't have a clue how to tell.

FATE, STRAIGHT UP

The demon's got him by the throat
Its claws are dug in deep and tight
I think he still could shake it off
But I won't rate the odds he might.

He's crewed on every kind of boat
From trawlers down to trollers
From quiet inside bays out to
The surging westward rollers.

Crabbing on the Bering Sea
Or longlining Southeast
He took on each job heartily
No fear his features creased

From hauling gear in fifty knots
To steering through a foggy murk
He greeted every challenge
As if it were his chosen work

And so it is. He loves the way
A boat's alive beneath your feet,
the smell and feel of flying spray
When hull and cresting wavetops meet

The fish cascading on the deck
The treasure growing in the hold
The pay, the honest pay that's his
When back in port the catch is sold

And ever with him goes the dream
Whose seed so long ago was sown
The dream of heading out to sea
On board a boat he calls his own

And one can see no reason why,
Considering all the work he's done
And learned so well, no reason why
It won't come true---excepting one:

The demon, waiting back in port
Behind each open barroom door
That lures him from his chosen course
And takes him in its grip once more

The lure of women, friendship, laughter,
Pleasures seldom found at sea
The feeling free of inhibition---
Who could say this shouldn't be?

Yet something in him cannot find
The line beyond which pain's in store
The line where reason drops away
And all that's left's the thirst for more

And even more, till numbness comes
And pleasure's lost, along with pain
Till waking up in some strange room
A hellish throbbing in his brain

So mired in the demon's thrall
The only course he knows to set
Is through the barroom door again
To get himself more wasted yet

Till finally he shows up drunk
To fumble at some shoreside chore
While his skipper's doubt increases---
His boat sails off, he's left ashore.

A familiar trend repeats itself
He knows his value, sells it clear
And soon he'll find another boat
To take him far away from here...

Now, is it free will makes this cycle
Or is it simply meant to be
That fate must wash us back and forth,
That from its force we're never free?

And if we are but Chance's playthings
Helpless born and soon to pass
Let's sympathize with who seeks solace
In the demon's glittering glass.

Dis Illusion

Sleeping, anchored near the beach
The finish of a record season
Tossing, thrashing fitfully
Though the wind is but a breeze

Shoals and shoals of tiny spirits
From the fish I'd caught that year
Skittered through my dreams and clamored
Outraged in my sleeping ear:

"Death too soon! To what end have you
Barred us from our spawning ground
Why such anger in the blows
Your gaff delivered---are you sound?"

With no answer, I dissembled
Turned away from summer's strife
Gave no further thought to slaughter
Slipped into my winter life.

Four months later, six miles higher,
Eastbound over North Atlantic,
Sense no signals from below, no
Salmon spirits, calm nor frantic

Still, I'm sure they're down there somewhere,
Though but handfuls, runs in slivers
Hanging on till human progress
Ebbs, and gives them back their rivers

Then, a hundred yards below
The Channel on a high speed train
Try again to pull in signals
Too much concrete? Tried in vain...

(Northward, in the fjords of Norway
Hordes of feeble pulses quicken
Are these farmfish really salmon?
Since each flies, is eagle chicken?

And the troller, lately hunter
Ranging after valued prey
Now, low-price high-volume fisher
Poultry farmer, in a way...)

Southern France: a supermarket
Frozen pen-reared fillets here
Price, ten dollars for a pound
I hold a chunk up to my ear

No vibrations, nothing lifelike
Neither in the fresh fish racks
Of wide-wale steaks, like farm-forced trees
Whose grain has form but substance lacks

Nor from the "Atlantique fume"
At thirty dollars to the pound
Too dear, too sad, I shamble on
Though losing faith, still casting 'round

Now, what in hell's this frozen carcass
Shrinkwrapped in its plastic seal
Freezer burned, and crystallized
But hefty, vital, somehow real

"*Sauvage d'Alaska*", $3 per pound
---something fishy here, I think
All's made clear down in the fine print
On the label: gillnet pink

Ah, France, so renowned for *coeur;*
For *liberte', fraternite';*
You've fallen for those glitzy-surfaced
Poultry-farm fish from Norway

America, your market skills
Still make the competition jumpy
But here's the champion you've found
To fight the farms: a net-caught humpy.

Too absurd, this masquerade
Where taste's forgotten, blandness praised
Of drug-fed mass-production frauds,
Caged, in listless boredom raised

Salmon lovers! Rise in anger
Storm the palates, seize the day
Drive these shadows off the table
Give us back our *qualite'*!

FOR MATT

The fleet's strung out along the hundred-fathom curve
Shut down and drifting for the night
The boats roll wildly in the choppy windswept sea
Mast lights arcing on the horizon

I watch the other lights, before I go to sleep
It's comforting to know there's friends out there
Companionship is vital on a sea so cold and deep
But now there's one less light on the horizon

And, God, it was a bright one, Matt
You sure knew how to shine
You always had a story
That you'd share to pass slow time
Your philosophic attitude
Was ever there at hand
For friends to whom the struggle
Could feel more than we could stand
Your ready wit, your curious mind,
Your conscientious view
Of what we're doing to our world
And what we ought to do...
Boy howdy, Matt, the radio
Seems empty without you.

I know your spirit's still around, and won't fade easily
I know you'll live on in our hearts and minds
And I hope to God you're sailing on some ocean I can't see---
But I still miss your light on the horizon.

AFTER YOU MISSED THE LAST BUS OUT OF WESTPORT

It's all right here, on the verge of the harbor:
All that you need to rebuild your dream.
A sudden cut in the tidal marsh
Dry at low tide with occasional pools
Clear as the air when the wind veers northwest
And strewn on the brown sandy bottom
The remains of small crabs and clams
Skeletal shroud for live buried brethren.

Above, on the bank, a fist of feathers
A bit of bone and a compact scat
And there, looping over the reeds, flies the predator
Hushing the odd bits of birdsong below.
Then, like a knife through the air, a gull's cry
The drone of a plane, the murmuring wind,
A hammer, the tires of home-driving tourists.

Just off the shore, a loon appears
Shivers its wings and dives again.
Farther out, vestigial seas
Reduced after crossing the Grays Harbor bar
Reborn as small breakers that chase one another
Across hidden sandbanks to weaken and die
Subsumed in the deeper blue water beyond.

Yards down the beach, two sad trollers conspire
Ungainly, abandoned, slowrotting away,
Days of full fish-holds now just a reverie
Planking and frames a haven for barnacles.

And the wind sighs low in the marshgrass
Small wavelets lick at the shore
The tide turns and makes its way back up the channel
Your heart fills with sorrow and hope.

REALITY ESCAPE

Whsh whsh whsh---an axe flies through the air
Bounces off a stanchion with a CLANG
Desperate footsteps clatter off somewhere
We're under assault by a desperate pirate gang.

Far up in the bow, gunfire breaks out
Two defenders hold off twenty-three
Blood-crazed attackers---now, with a shout
Their leader falls, with a bullet to the knee...

It's movie time aboard the Northern Pride
Which is any time the gear's not being run
Any movie's good, if it's got homicide
And the volume's turned up high enough to stun

There's a video on in every common space---
Wheelhouse, galley, staterooms---save the head...
Though who knows why, coz it's the perfect place
Why sit bored, you could watch a cartoon instead

I'm in the galley, amidst the blood and gore
Of a truly creepy modern vampire flick
With punctured neck, the heroine's feeling sore
I'm feeling there's a chance I might get sick.

It came on while I was lying in my berth
In the boat's best cabin, where I've been assigned--
It has to be the cabin of greatest worth,
Cause it's farthest in the front? Well, I don't mind

Though we're bucking into a violent westerly swell
Pitching up and down like a carnival ride
I'm still honored, because I can tell
This space once belonged to some bona fide

Celebrity; at least that's what I conclude
From the wafer thin state of the mattress foam---
It's clear some truly gigantic dude
Like JR Sweezy of the Seahawks called this home.

Still, I could have slept, I was that tired,
But for the noisy flick my mate had on the screen...
If they gave out an Oscar for most gunshots fired,
This western would've had the prize clean

Now I notice the bow's begun pitching
With an even more vigorous amplitude---
Still, there's no need yet to start bitching
Use the fishermen's mantra, "it's all attitude."

I'm grooving on the ride, till my euphoria snaps
I glance at the TV---it's no longer there
A sharp wave has broken it free of its straps
And, after doing a back flip in mid-air

Crash! It lands on the deck right by my bunk.
The screen's still bright; the shots still banging out,
But now I'm slipping into a serious funk
'Cause the lashing that held it in place was really stout

For it to break, the seas must be really rough,
Considering this is an Aleutian longline boat...
I re-mount the TV, then decide that's enough
As the queasiness starts to rise in my throat...

Time to find a spot that's a little more stable.
Back aft, here's this stupid Dracula remake
But I slide into a seat at the galley table
Hoping the motion might be easier to take.

A couple other crew are wedged in here
Spellbound by the movie's bloodsoaked action
I really wish I could shift into their gear
But though I try, I can't find the attraction

The acting's lame, the plot moves slow as sludge---
No way can I suspend my disbelief
But no way, either, can I judge
Whatever brings these other guys relief

Cause well I know, this fishery is brutal
Especially here, along the Aleutian chain
Where often all the effort just seems futile
A constant scene of working against the grain

Sometimes you run out set after set
Without getting more than a skimpy haul
And if you do land on the fish, you can bet
There's a chance you'll wind up with nothing at all

Cause the current's constantly trying to drag
Your buoys down never to rise again
And even if you get the tides in the bag
And pull up a string full of butts, that's when

You find you've set on a giant pile
Of sand fleas---the fish come up just skin and bones.
And if you avoid bugs, there's creatures <u>more</u> vile
That bring from the crew these terrible groans

Those freaking whales! It's guaranteed they'll pick
Every last fish before it gets to the top
Then they'll hang around waiting for you to stick
Your gear out again for their next meal---stop!

That's enough---it's a rough go, no doubt
So if the crew wants to use their short time off
To escape into a movie and just space out
I'm sure not one who's qualified to scoff

As a walk-on quota holder from Southeast
Who also fishes a troller, by the way
I'm viewed with skepticism, to say the least
These guys are sure that trolling's nothing but play.

Trollers spend their days casually driving around
Sometimes taking a king salmon off the line
Then at night, set anchor in sheltered ground
For a well-planned supper (paired with a perfect wine)...

And after a peaceful night of easy dreams
A leisurely breakfast, then out to try it again...
All right, I know that's just how it seems
To these guys---there's plenty times when

I've jogged upwind, through a long rough night;
Stayed up past one a.m. icing my catch
Got up again in two hours, before the first light
To be harassed all day by a rapacious batch

Of thieving sea lions---but I won't convince
Any longliners with some such defensive report
All I can do is try hard not to wince
When they say trolling's 'a gentlemen's sport.'

What I can do, to avoid more ridicule
Is, now, do my absolute best not to puke
I've got to keep up the appearance of cool
If I'm to avoid sarcasm and rebuke

I've got to get adjusted to this motion.
I know---I'll attain a Zen-like state:
It's all one world...it's all the same ocean...
Rough or calm, why differentiate

Turn off your mind, relax and float downstream
Tap into that inner zone of calm
Life is just part of an everlasting dream...
I'm almost there, when someone drops a bomb

Into my zone. The cook has started work
On lunch. Onto a fiery hot griddle
He dumps some oil. My innards twist and jerk
As a greasy cloud develops in the middle

Of the galley, and gets me in its sights.
Could I escape? Head on back to bed?
Too late. Obscuring the overhead lights,
The thickening smoke comes and settles around my head.

All the gains I'd made evaporate
Cold sweat collects to glisten on my brow
The nausea begins to escalate
Humiliation seems inevitable now

Then a plate's dropped on the table with a *crack!*
And there, below my desperate eyes
A pair of greasy crab cakes staring back
And a fork. My God. What a grim surprise

A straw that'll surely break the camel's spine.
But hold on now, isn't this the big red king
That came aboard on last night's final line?
Caught, somehow, on a circle hook, a thing

Of improbable beauty, all of us agreed
Now minced up well and mixed with egg and flour
A tasty-looking dish, one must concede
Maybe my future's not really all that sour

I try a bite---oh man, it's heaven-sent
Two more, my well-being regains traction,
By the time I clean the plate, I'm totally content
And leaning back in utter satisfaction

My reputation's saved for one more day
Even vampires can't disturb my gastric peace
It's like that old blues singer used to say
Ain't nothing really good without the grease.

No Spring for the Fisherman

April coming strong, the long winter's over
It's like someone pulled off the coffin lid
Soon you'll be outdoors, barefoot in clover
Pulling out your backpack, hiking off the grid

Free to make love without three quilts and a blanket
Dance around the yard, your domestic Serengeti
Take your music outside, and really crank it
Grab the mountain bike and ride till you're sweaty

It's time for joy and rebirth, now we've got to spring
Time for thawing out your inward-spiraled soul
But hold on, you've forgotten one small thing
In three weeks the season starts---and you are in a hole

All that boat work you put off, since tying up last fall
No May day party for you, best get your ass in gear
You'll have to go in overdrive to take care of it all
In time to make the starting date---oh man, it's almost here!

Get that oil change done, tune up and run the rack
Clean the bilge and paint the deck, change the trolling wire
New bulbs in the running lights, chip rust off the stack
Freak out cause your license is about to expire

Haul out and paint the hull, check the zincs and shaft
Check the thru hulls check the bearing check the davit mounts
Test the radar, test the EPIRB, certify the raft
Check the hydro system, check your bank account---

Whoa, it's empty! Guess that's it, all you can afford
Must be time to go...maybe you can get ice
And groceries on credit, then pull the lines aboard
Head out for the grounds, and make that sacrifice

Of all the fun you could've had in spring and summer
If you didn't have to work for months until the fall
And the rain's return...yeah, it is a bummer
But no one forced you in this life---it *was* your call.

Let's time travel forward, twenty years or so
Your life's taken a major turn, as you've decided
To try a different job---you've given up the show
Sold out, after family and fishing collided

With young kids at home, those five months away
You'd never see again, not time you could borrow
And pay back in the autumn. Each lost summer day
Was gone for good, would never replay tomorrow

And so you made the change, found work close to home
The springs and summers filled with family fun
River rafting through the boisterous rapids' foam
Endless games of catch, the high school game's home run

Swimming in the lake, and campfires in the night
Hoops out in the driveway, a pony in the field
All of it added up to a life that felt just right
Became the newer normal, as every spring revealed

The path you'd taken was, clearly, the best choice
Comparison was foolish, the differences were vast
Nothing to be gained, in ever giving voice
To doubts about those things you'd left in the past---

The sharp anticipation sailing into the sea's unknown
Each trip a grand adventure, a challenge to be met
Win or lose, it's all on you and your crew alone
And when you win, the self-regard's as good as it can get

The brilliant starry nights offshore, far from city light
Air so fresh and clear, it's a pleasure to inhale
That first king of the season, flashing silver bright
The measure of your skill, read out on the weigh-up scale

It was good, but you got to take its loss with grace
Compared to the warmth you get from your family's touch
Compared to the springtime sun at home that took its place...
It wasn't all <u>that</u> good...you don't miss it...no...*not much*.

YOU MAKE YOUR OWN LUCK

You make your own luck
was always your credo.

It seemed it could be true
watching you truck
around the neighborhood in that XK140...
and no one excels in water polo
If they're given to self doubt

We met in an LA rainstorm
rolling in the mud
with a slippery football
and some other jocks you knew
Our opposites attracted
you the doer
I the dreamer
became like brothers
young horns locked
in everything we did:
who can drink to crazy
　who revs farthest above the redline
　　who tries hardest to win every game
　　　who goes home with the girl

You make your own luck
is what you always believed.

But there were forces to contend with
that truly foolish war
with its spurious propaganda
turned us into rebels
derailing the careers
that otherwise
might have swallowed us

Busting out of school
we put our credentials
to hopeful, ridiculous use

You took your MBA
into a high school classroom
tried to inoculate your kids
against the pestilence of lies
raining down from above
I applied my psych degree
to riders in my midnight taxi
comforting the lonely
          the drunk
                    and the chronically sad
with a swift smooth chase
down dark deserted city streets

You make your own luck
is what you always figured.

You pressed it past the limit
of the school district's tolerance
creating revolutionaries
not what they had in mind
as they pushed you out

you slammed the door
and made it back to Seattle
where our lives took a hard
and beautiful right turn
when you discovered fishing.

With an inappropriate boat
and a bucket full of hope
you set out on the rumor
of salmon off the coast
I went with you one day
in a washboard cross swell
the fish were phoning it in
over fourteen long hours
we only hooked three
but that was all it took
I loved every rain soaked moment
and back on the beach
like a newly-hooked junkie
I could have no other thought
till I got a troller of my own.

You always thought
that *you make your own luck*.

It was easy to believe
as you brought in deckloads
defied the vilest weather
and made it back to harbor
(though sometimes at the end
of a long tow line...)

We stayed gloriously immersed
as the seasons ebbed and flooded

and though we took diverging courses
through our shoreside lives
the sea remained our bond
though we fished long miles apart
It was always good to know
your wheel and mine
were churning the same water.

You often suggested
that *we make our own luck.*

I got the word one day
of your last unlucky break
as I strove against the odds
to salvage a terrible season
trolling for groundfish, all alone
out on an offshore bank

The news cut deep into my soul
on that sharp September morning
sharp as the ling cods' razor teeth
sharp as the stabbing greedy beaks
of shearwaters squabbling off the stern
I pulled my gear aboard
and never more returned
to that luck-forsaken spot

There have been times in my life
I was into that Ayn Rand willpower jive
marry it with a share of compassion
it's as good a code as any I suppose

But there is force beyond our will
as there are sudden violent winds
and lives that run on hubris
find their end, like any other

We make our own luck
we always wanted to imagine.

And what I'm left to imagine now
along with your last brave struggle
to get at the failing pump
buried beneath a ton of tuna
sharp waves breaking over the rail
the stern drinking deep and settling low
the bow nosing up, then finally subsiding...

And what I'm left to imagine now
is that you might have designed your death
with the same will
you so exuberantly applied to life
that perhaps at least one of your final thoughts
out in the coal black midnight water
as she headed for the bottom
there in a thousand fathoms
was "Wow---that is really something,
how her running lights keep burning"

I still imagine them, now and then,
how they somehow went on burning
willfully burning, red and green.

PORPOISES

As Cameron sailed on the sea one day
He heard a voice in the water say
"Oh, man. What a bummer!
Are we in a mess.
We've goofed it up big time on this one, I guess."

Now what was all this? Cam ran to the bow.
He leaned out as far as the rail would allow
And there down below
Seven porpoises swam.
They said, "Hey! Who're you?" And Cam said, "I'm Cam!"

"We're Adolph One, Adolph Two...so on, through Seven.
Just call us by number. Except Three---he's Kevin."
And with that they went back
To complaining: "Aw, rats.
Stinky clams! Why'd we go and lose sight of those cats?"

"What's the problem?" asked Cam. "Perhaps I can help."
Two snickered, "what help could you be, just a whelp?"
"Not so fast," argued Four.
"Let's go think on it."
Cam watched them swim off, quick as lickety-split.

But soon they were back. "Okay, Cam. Can you ride?"
"On horses I can," replied Cam with some pride.
"You'll do, then. Let's go!
We can talk on the way."
Cam jumped on Five's back, and the group streaked away.

"Here's the hassle," said One. We were s'posed to deliver
A herd of catfish to a guy in Manx River.
We were doing just fine
Till some herring swam by.
If there's one thing that we love, it's herring. Oh, my!

"We forgot about catfish; we all stuffed ourselves.
Our bellies swole up from size six to size twelves.
And when the last herring
Was gone, we looked 'round---
But by then there wasn't one cat to be found!

So that's how it happened. Our jobs are at stake.
Help us track down those catfish. Please, we need a break!"
Said Cam, "Sure I will.
I will give it a try.
I'm very well known for my sharpness of eye."

So off on their search through the ocean they swam,
Adolphs Seven through One, and Kevin, and Cam.
They made quite a sight
As they sped on their way.
Such leaping, such splashing, such throwing of spray!

They searched and they searched, till at Latitude 3
Cam shouted, "By whiskers! What's that I see?
Way, way over yonder---"
And he grinned like a gator---
"It's your catfish, I bet, down there by the equator!"

Sure enough, he was right, so they circled the school.
With kelp for a whip, Cam kept the cats cool
As they drove them back north
And they sang as they herded
An old catboy song, somewhat wistfully worded---

"Sushi fry, fry O
Git along little catfish
It's your misfortune
And none of my own.

Sushi fry, fry O
Git along you sea kittens
A plate with hush puppies
Will be your new home."

They drove right along, past the reefs of Aruba,
Through sunny warm seas off Jamaica and Cuba,
And though often some herring
Would pass in a bunch
They kept to their work without one stop for lunch.

Then, up near the Gulf Coast, Cam's boat came in sight.
Five said, "Thanks a lot---I'm sure now we're all right."
Cam climbed back aboard
And he hauled up his sails
And his friends said goodbye with a splash of their tails.

Feeling sad at the end of this porpoiseful trip
Cam stood by the helm of his stout little ship.
Then he set a new course,
And he stretched, and he grinned
For there's surely adventure, wherever there's wind.

Other books by R A Bard:

"West of Spencer"
   A novel, set along the Gulf of Alaska coast, about a Sitka salmon troller coping with unreliable girlfriends, even less reliable fish, and drinking companions who persist in inflicting on him their ideas about oboe concertos and Kantian logic, all of which make getting tossed around on the ocean in violent weather seem attractive in comparison.

"Red Flags in Blue Water"
   A collection of voyages taken as a boat delivery captain on various oceans--jobs that went south due to either belligerent weather, the stubborn disintegration of mechanical systems, or crew behavior that cries out for psychiatric help.

Published by Smooth Passage Books and available at independent bookstores or on Amazon by way of the author page for R A Bard

https://www.amazon.com/R-A-Bard/e/B00PIQWGNA